W9-DGF-528

1/2019
Wl

States ARIZONA

by Jason Kirchner

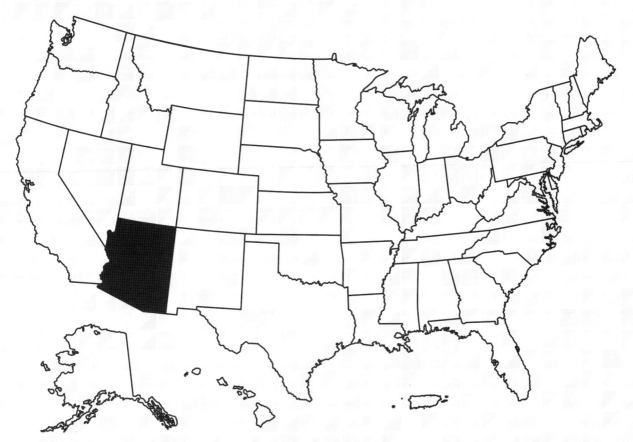

CAPSTONE PRESS
a capstone imprint

Next Page Books are published by Capstone Press,
1710 Roe Crest Drive, North Mankato, Minnesota 56003
www.mycapstone.com

Library of Congress Cataloging-in-Publication Data
Cataloging-in-publication information is on file with the Library of
Congress.
ISBN 978-1-5157-0389-1 (library binding)
ISBN 978-1-5157-0449-2 (paperback)
ISBN 978-1-5157-0501-7 (ebook PDF)

Editorial Credits
Jaclyn Jaycox, editor; Katy LaVigne, designer; Morgan Walters,
media researcher; Laura Manthe, production specialist

Photo Credits
Alamy: PureStock, bottom right 20; Capstone Press: Angi Gahler, map
4, 7; CriaImages.com: Robert Nash Collection, bottom 18; Dreamstime:
Milahelp S.r.o. Milahelp S.r.o., top right 21; Library of Congress:
Robert S. Oakes, top 19, Smithsonian Report, 27; National Archives
and Records Administration, middle 18; Newscom: Everett Collection,
top 18, PETE SOUZA/KRT, bottom 19, Reinhard, H./picture alliance/
Arco Images G, middle left 21; One Mile Up, Inc., (flag, seal) 22-23;
Shutterstock: Anton Foltin, bottom right 8, Anton Foltin, 11, Erik
Harrison, cover, Everett Historical, 26, Francesco R. Iacomino, 7,
Joseph Sohm, top 24, Marisa Estivill, 10, Martha Marks, bottom left
20, Matt Jeppson, top left 21, Mike Liu, bottom 24, milosk50, 6, Nagel
Photography, 13, Oscity, 15, Paul B. Moore, 17, Peter Kunasz, 9,
Rainbohm, top right 20, Ronnie Chua, 16, Rusty Dodson, middle right
21, s_bukley, middle 19, Shriram Patki, bottom left 8, somchaij, 5, Tim
Roberts Photography, 14, Tom Grundy, bottom right 21, Tutti Frutti,
bottom left 21, You Touch Pix of EuToch, top left 20; Wikimedia: Billy
Hathorn, 25, Frederic Remington, 12, Roosewelt Pinheiro/ABr, 28,
Titoxd, 29

All design elements by Shutterstock

Printed and bound in China.
0316/CA21600187
012016   009436F16

TABLE OF CONTENTS

Want to take your research further? Ask your librarian if your school subscribes to PebbleGo Next. If so, when you see this helpful symbol 🔾 throughout the book, log onto www.pebblegonext.com for bonus downloads and information.

LOCATION

Arizona is one of the southwestern states. Arizona has five neighbors. North of Arizona is Utah. New Mexico lies to the east. Nevada and California are on the west. To the south is the country of Mexico. The Colorado River forms most of Arizona's western border. Phoenix is near the center of the state. It is Arizona's capital and largest city. Arizona's next largest cities are Tucson, Mesa, Chandler, and Glendale.

PebbleGo Next Bonus!
To print and label your own map, go to
www.pebblegonext.com
and search keywords:
AZ MAP

Horseshoe Bend is formed by the Colorado River, located near Page, Arizona.

GEOGRAPHY

Land regions in Arizona include the Colorado Plateau, the Transition Zone, and the Sonoran Desert. The Colorado Plateau lies in northern Arizona. It is a high, mostly flat area with some of the most colorful rocks in North America. The Transition Zone is a narrow strip of land southwest of the Colorado Plateau. Several mountain ranges are in this rocky region. Humphreys Peak in north-central Arizona is the highest point in Arizona. It is 12,633 feet (3,851 meters) above sea level. The famous Grand Canyon is also in northern Arizona. The Sonoran Desert covers much of southwestern Arizona. The desert has river valleys, sand dunes, and inactive volcanoes.

The Grand Canyon is the United States' 15th oldest national park.

The sandstone rock formation called The Wave is located on the Colorado Plateau..

Legend
- ▲ Highest Point
- ◯ Lake
- ▢ National Park
- 〰 River

Grand Canyon National Park

Colorado River

Lake Mead

COLORADO PLATEAU

TRANSITION ZONE

Humphreys Peak

Petrified Forest National Park

Verde River

Colorado River

Salt River

Theodore Roosevelt Lake

Gila River

Gila River

SONORAN DESERT

Saguaro National Park

Tumacacori National Historic Park

N
W E
S

Gulf of California

Scale
Miles
0   25   50   100   125
0 25 50 75 100
Kilometers

WEATHER

Arizona's mountains and plateaus are cool all year. Summers in the desert are hot. The average summer temperature in Arizona is 78 degrees Fahrenheit (26 degrees Celsius). The average winter temperature is 43°F (6°C).

Average High and Low Temperatures (Phoenix, AZ)

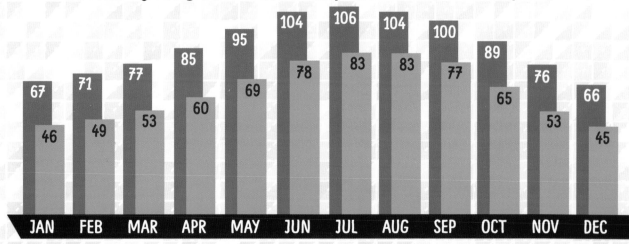

Month	High	Low
JAN	67	46
FEB	71	49
MAR	77	53
APR	85	60
MAY	95	69
JUN	104	78
JUL	106	83
AUG	104	83
SEP	100	77
OCT	89	65
NOV	76	53
DEC	66	45

London Bridge

London Bridge was originally built in London, England. It now stretches over Lake Havasu in western Arizona. Piece by piece, the bridge was taken apart in London. Then workers put it back together in Arizona.

Petrified Forest

The Petrified Forest is located in the Painted Desert in northeastern Arizona. It is the world's largest collection of petrified wood. Millions of years ago, rivers dumped huge trees on the land. Over millions of years, the trees turned into stone. The trees turned into red, orange, and green rock.

The Grand Canyon

The Grand Canyon in northern Arizona is one of the biggest canyons in the world. Visitors can stand near the canyon's edge to view the red, purple, and brown rock. At the bottom, 1 mile (1.6 kilometers) below, lies the Colorado River. Over millions of years, this fast-flowing river carved the steep cliffs to form the rocky display.

HISTORY AND GOVERNMENT

Francisco Vásquez de Coronado led an expedition from Mexico to Kansas, where he discovered the Grand Canyon and the Colorado River.

Native people lived in Arizona for thousands of years. Spanish explorers were the first Europeans in Arizona. Explorer Francisco Vásquez de Coronado claimed Arizona for Spain in 1540. In 1752 Spaniards built their first permanent settlement at Tubac. Mexico gained independence from Spain in 1821. Arizona then belonged to Mexico. The United States won most of Arizona from Mexico in 1848 after winning the Mexican War (1846–1848). In 1853 the United States bought a small area of land in southern Arizona from Mexico. Arizona Territory was created in 1863. In 1912 Arizona became the 48th state.

Arizona's government is made up of three branches. The governor is the leader of the executive branch, which carries out laws. The legislature makes laws. It is made up of the 30-member Senate and the 60-member House of Representatives. Judges and their courts make up the judicial branch. They uphold the laws.

Arizona's original state capitol building in Phoenix is now a museum.

INDUSTRY

Service industries are the largest industries in Arizona. About 85 percent of Arizona's workers are in service industries. They include health care, real estate, restaurants, and tourism. Tourism brings billions of dollars into the state. Millions of people visit Arizona's national parks and other attractions every year.

Manufacturing is also an important part of the state's economy. Most of Arizona's manufacturing is in high-technology products such as computer parts, cell phones, and aircraft parts.

Intel Corporation has a plant in Chandler, Arizona, and is one of the city's largest employers.

Arizona's mountains have many minerals. The state leads the nation in mining copper. Arizona's mines also produce gold and silver.

Farmland covers more than one-third of Arizona's land. Ranchers raise cattle in many parts of Arizona. During summer farmers grow cotton in south-central Arizona. Lettuce is grown during winter in southwestern Arizona.

The Hoover Dam was built to control flooding of the Colorado River, provide irrigation, and produce hydroelectric power.

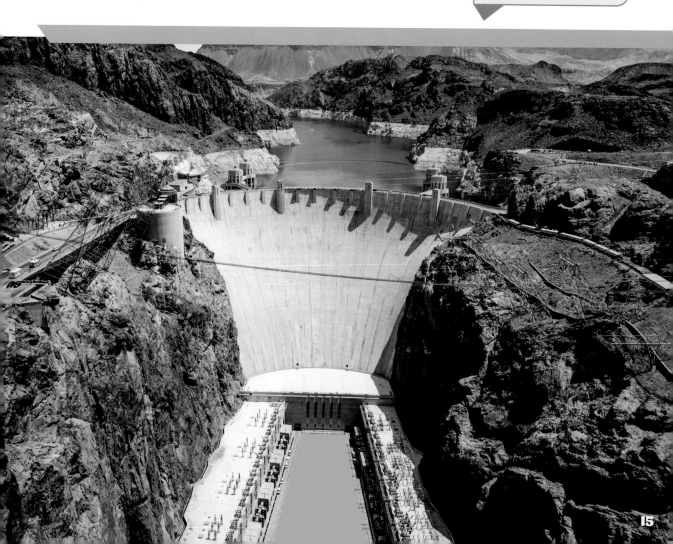

POPULATION

American Indians lived in Arizona thousands of years before Spanish and other European settlers came. Today more than 25 percent of Arizona's land is covered by Indian reservations. About 4 percent of Arizonans are American Indian. The largest American Indian group in Arizona is the Navajo Nation. The Navajo reservation takes up most of northeastern Arizona and reaches into New Mexico and Utah. It is the largest Indian reservation in the country.

Population by Ethnicity

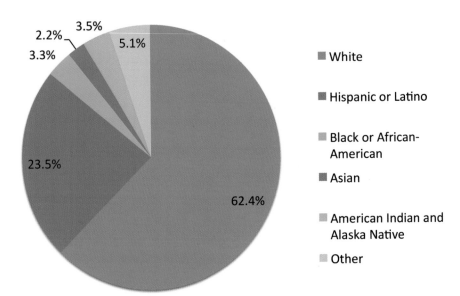

- 3.5%
- 2.2%
- 3.3%
- 5.1%
- 23.5%
- 62.4%

- ■ White
- ■ Hispanic or Latino
- ■ Black or African-American
- ■ Asian
- ■ American Indian and Alaska Native
- ■ Other

Source: U.S. Census Bureau.

White people make up more than half of Arizona's population. About 30 percent of Arizona's residents are Hispanic. They belong to Mexican and other Spanish-speaking cultures. About 4 percent of Arizona's population is African-American. Asians make up about 3 percent of the state's people.

Native Americans are invited to participate in the Heard Museum World Championship Hoop Dance Contest in Phoenix each year.

PebbleGo Next Bonus! To watch a video about ancient petroglyphs and Monument Valley, go to www.pebblegonext.com and search keywords:
AZ VIDEO

FAMOUS PEOPLE

Cesar Chavez (1927–1993) was a labor leader who worked for the rights of farmworkers, especially Mexican migrant workers. He organized the United Farm Workers union and gained workers' rights through boycotts and strikes.

Charles Poston (1825–1902) is called the "Father of Arizona." He was a miner. In 1864 he became Arizona Territory's first representative in the U.S. Congress.

Geronimo (1829–1909) was a Chiricahua Apache chief who led his people in fighting the U.S. government over rights to land. Geronimo escaped many captures but finally surrendered in 1886. He was born along the present-day Arizona-New Mexico border.

William Rehnquist (1924–2005) became an associate justice of the U.S. Supreme Court in 1972 and chief justice in 1986. He worked as a lawyer in Phoenix from 1953 to 1969.

Emma Stone (1988–) is an actress. She has appeared in *Crazy, Stupid, Love* (2011), *The Help* (2011), and *Gangster Squad* (2013). She was born in Scottsdale.

Sandra Day O'Connor (1930–) is a retired United States Supreme Court justice. In 1981 she became the first woman associate justice of the U.S. Supreme Court. She became an assistant attorney general of Arizona in 1965. She also served two terms in the Arizona Senate.

STATE SYMBOLS

Tree

palo verde

Flower

saguaro blossom

Bird

cactus wren

Fish

Apache trout

PebbleGo Next Bonus! To make a popular southwestern snack, go to www.pebblegonext.com and search keywords: **AZ RECIPE**

Amphibian

Arizona tree frog

Gemstone

turquoise

Mammal

ringtail

Reptile

Arizona ridge-nosed rattlesnake

Fossil

petrified wood

Butterfly

two-tailed swallowtail

FAST FACTS

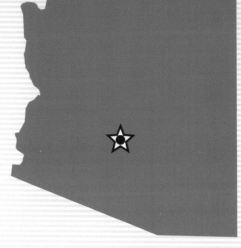

STATEHOOD
1912

CAPITAL ☆
Phoenix

LARGEST CITY •
Phoenix

SIZE
113,594 square miles (294,207 square kilometers)
land area (2010 U.S. Census Bureau)

POPULATION
6,626,624 (2013 U.S. Census estimate)

STATE NICKNAME
Grand Canyon State

STATE MOTTO
"Ditat Deus," which is Latin for "God enriches"

STATE SEAL

The mountains and sunrise represent the landscape of Arizona. The dam, lake, and irrigated field show that Arizonans have to water their land to grow crops. The miner represents the importance of mining to the state. "Ditat Deus" is the state's motto. At the bottom of the seal, 1912 represents when Arizona became a state.

PebbleGo Next Bonus! To print and color your own flag, go to www.pebblegonext.com and search keywords:

AZ FLAG

STATE FLAG

The 13 stripes at the top of Arizona's flag stand for the 13 original American colonies. The stripes look like a sunset. The blue on the bottom of the flag is the same color of blue on the U.S. flag. The copper star in the center stands for Arizona's copper mines.

MINING PRODUCTS

copper, molybdenum, coal

MANUFACTURED GOODS

computer and electronic products, transportation equipment, food products, chemicals, fabricated metal products, machinery

FARM PRODUCTS

beef cattle, cotton, lettuce, citrus fruits, dairy products

PROFESSIONAL SPORTS TEAMS

Arizona Rattlers (AFL)
Arizona Diamondbacks (MLB)
Phoenix Suns (NBA)
Phoenix Mercury (WNBA)
Arizona Cardinals (NFL)
Phoenix Coyotes (NHL)

PebbleGo Next Bonus!
To learn the lyrics to
the state song, go to
www.pebblegonext.com
and search keywords:

AZ SONG

ARIZONA TIMELINE

1400s The Navajo and the Apache Indians come to Arizona. The Navajo live in the northeast. The Apache live in the mountains to the south.

1540 Spanish explorer Francisco Vásquez de Coronado leads an expedition into Arizona and claims it for Spain.

1620 The Pilgrims establish a colony in the New World in present-day Massachusetts.

1691 Father Eusebio Francisco Kino arrives in Arizona from Mexico. He starts many churches called missions in southern Arizona.

1821 Mexico gains independence from Spain. Arizona becomes part of Mexico.

1848 After the Mexican War (1846–1848), the United States receives most of Arizona.

1861–1865 The Union and the Confederacy fight the Civil War.

1863 Arizona becomes a U.S. territory.

1864
Colonel Kit Carson and his troops force several thousand Navajo Indians to march more than 300 miles (483 kilometers) from Arizona to New Mexico. Many Navajo die during this march. The Navajo call the journey the Long Walk.

1869
American John Wesley Powell explores the Colorado River through Arizona's Grand Canyon.

1912
Arizona becomes the 48th state on February 14.

1914–1918
World War I is fought; the United States enters the war in 1917.

1919 Grand Canyon National Park is established in northern Arizona.

1973 The Central Arizona Project begins. The project brings water from the Colorado River to the deserts of southern Arizona. The entire project costs more than $4 billion.

1974 Attorney, judge, and ambassador Raul Castro is elected Arizona's first Hispanic governor.

1981 Sandra Day O'Connor of Arizona is the first woman on the U.S. Supreme Court.

1998   Former Secretary of State Jane Dee Hull becomes the first woman elected governor of Arizona.

2010   A dam at Tempe Town Lake in Tempe bursts. Nearly 1 billion gallons (3.8 million liters) of lake water drains into the Salt River. The lake is closed to the public for three months.

2012   Arizona celebrates 100 years of statehood on February 14.

2015   Copper becomes the official state metal.

Glossary

canyon *(KAN-yuhn)*—a deep, narrow valley

carve *(KAHRV)*—to cut a shape out of a piece of wood, stone, or other substance

executive *(ig-ZE-kyuh-tiv)*—the branch of government that makes sure laws are followed

industry *(IN-duh-stree)*—a business that produces a product or provides a service

irrigate *(IHR-uh-gate)*—to supply water for crops using channels or pipes

legislature *(LEJ-iss-lay-chur)*—a group of elected officials who have the power to make or change laws for a country or state

petrified *(PET-ruh-fide)*—a material that water and minerals have changed into stone or a stony subtance

peninsula *(puh-NIN-suh-luh)*—a piece of land that is surrounded by water on three sides

permanent *(PUR-muh-nuhnt)*—lasting for a long time, or forever

plateau *(pla-TOH)*—an area of high, flat land

region *(REE-juhn)*—a large area

Read More

Derzipilski, Kathleen. *Arizona*. It's My State! New York: Cavendish Square Pub., 2016.

Ganeri, Anita. *United States of America: A Benjamin Blog and His Inquisitive Dog Guide.* Country Guides. Chicago: Heinemann Raintree, 2015.

Hirsch, Rebecca. *What's Great About Arizona?* Our Great States. Minneapolis: Lerner Publications, 2015.

Internet Sites

FactHound offers a safe, fun way to find Internet sites related to this book. All of the sites on FactHound have been researched by our staff.

Here's all you do:

Visit *www.facthound.com*

Type in this code: 9781515703891

Check out projects, games and lots more at
www.capstonekids.com

Critical Thinking Using the Common Core

1. How does the weather differ between the mountains and the desert in Arizona? (Key Ideas and Details)

2. There are three land regions that make up Arizona. What are the differences in landscapes for each region? (Key Ideas and Details)

3. At one time, people thought Arizona was just a useless desert. Describe some of the ways in which Arizona is an important state. (Integration of Knowledge and Ideas)

Index